MW00980245

as a small child when my white cat, who liked to venture far afie
ne back home with fleas. The tiny insects soon appeared on my mo
bare legs, where our large white cat used to like to go to "caress h
f". When my mother consulted the family doctor, he asked if we ha
, and then suggested that we get rid of the cat. It was the end of
ld. My father went to the veterinarian's and returned with a powder
our of milk chocolate and instructions to spread it over the our ca
. On the first attempt, my father only half succeeded in covering
with the terrible chestnut coloured mixture. But Melon (our cat), pre

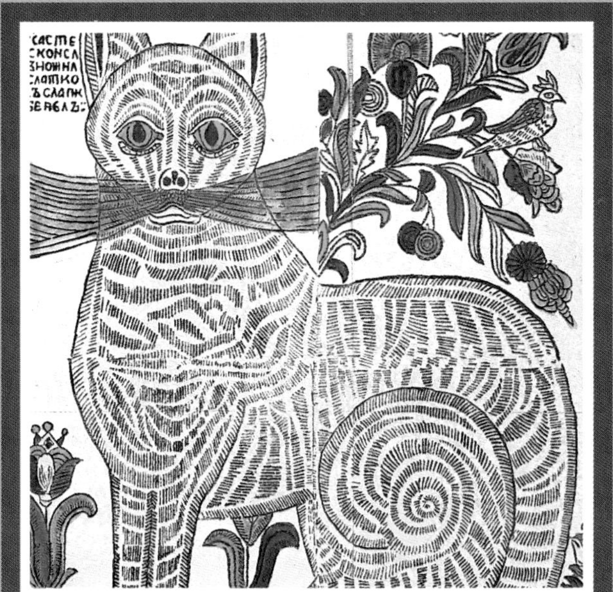

oled.
d, he
e back
r of
ner to
ered w
came
It wa
e cou
. Seve
where
nder
ure t
and h

at the same time. Melon looked every bit as beautiful as ever, but
t presence seemed to carry blame, and it shattered my little girl's hea
years went by, I owned other cats, but Melon remained the mythi
of my childhood, a bittersweet memory, similar to the memory of t
and the torments it can bring. I was a small child when my white c
liked to venture far afield, came back home with fleas. The t
cts soon appeared on my mother's bare legs, where our large white
d to like to go to "caress himself". When my mother consulted the fa

I was a small child when my white cat, who liked to venture far a

came back home with fleas. The tiny insects soon appeared on my mo

bare legs, where our large white cat used to like to go to "caress him

When my mother consulted the family doctor, he asked if we had a

and then suggested that we get rid of the cat. It was the end of the w

My father went to the veterinarian's and returned with a powder the c

of mi

he fi

errib

white

ried

fast.

ater,

nerve

quiet

were.

hat

at o

lear.

'disa

I tur

dour,

spirit

ime.

seem.

py, I

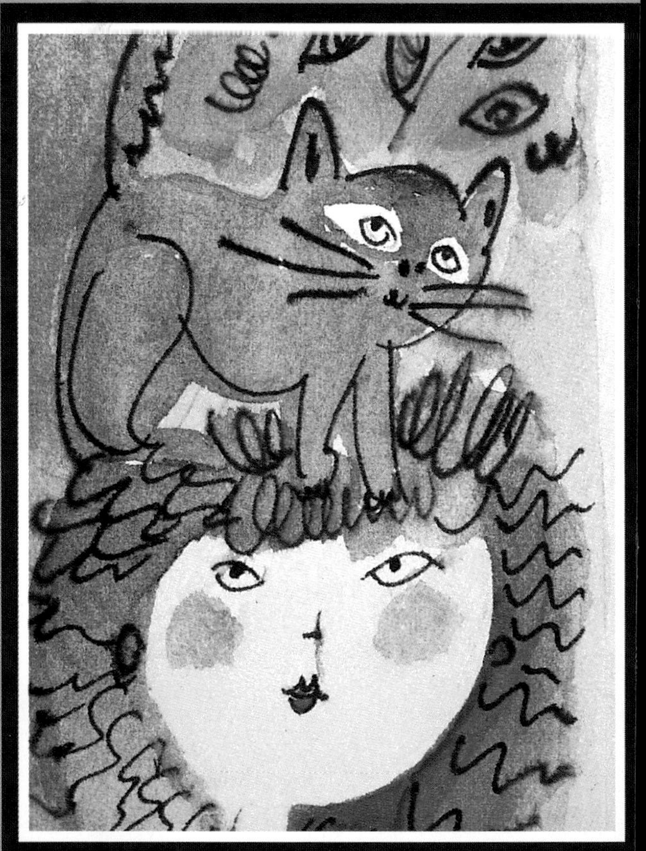

hood, a bittersweet memory, similar to the memory of true love and th

ments it can bring. I was a small child when my white cat, who liked to

ure far afield, came back home with fleas. The tiny insects

appeared on my mother's bare legs, where our large white cat used

o go to "caress himself". When my mother consulted the family doc

I love my
Cat

This book belongs to

_____

© 2000 MV Publishing Inc.
All rights reserved.

Published by:
MV Publishing Inc.
2565 Broadway, Suite 161
New York, New York 10025

Translated from the French by: Brenda O'Brien
Cover: Marc Alain
Graphic Design: Marc Alain

Picture Credits Cover 1 and 4: ©SuperStock
Picture Credits Page 1: ©Explorer, Paris/SuperStock;
Page 2: ©SuperStock; Pages 3 and 5: ©Peter Sickles/SuperStock;
Page 48: ©SuperStock

Legal Deposit: 2nd Quarter, 2000
National Library of Québec
National Library of Canada
National Library of France

Canadian Cataloguing in Publication Data
Therrien, Laurette
    I love my cat
    (Heartfelt series)
    Translation of: J'aime mon chat
    ISBN 2-89523-023-4
    1. Cats. 2. Cats - Pictorial works. I. Title.
    II. Series.
SF446.T4313 2000   636.8'0022'2   C00-940563-1

Canadä We acknowledge the financial support of the Government
of Canada through the Book Publishing Industry Development
Program (BPIDP) for our publishing activities.

I love my Cat

Laurette Therrien

MV Publishing

"God created the cat to allow humans the joy of caressing the tiger."

Joseph Méry (1798-1866)

Whether it be the smallest of house cats, so timid and so engaging, or the biggest alley cats, with injuries severe enough to give it a certain authority, the "mewing crew", felis domestica, is sociable and fully capable of demonstrating affection and at times, the most unexpected and unearned of caresses.

However, while well-tamed and a fast friend of humans, the cat remains totally independent and no one can possibly teach it to live other than freely and in dignity.

Since time immemorial, cats have been our constant companions. Their ability to communicate with us gives them a value that lions, panthers, leopards and other big cats will never have in our eyes. Yet they are all of the same ilk: they all belong to the Felidae, the cat family. They are all more or less wild. Naturally, when we see a tiny tiger or an adorable ocelot, our first reaction is to reach out to pet it, to run our hand over its soft fur. Yet caution makes us aware that some degree of danger is involved.

The reason is simple: because of its wild nature and because we have not been able to tame it, the tiger is a source of fear. On the other hand, the house cat is a source of comfort, though it shares many traits with its cousins.

A living paradox, the domestic cat — quiet, affectionate, charismatic — reassures us with its willing friendship, especially at times when we feel particularly alone.

A Relationship of Passion

One day an alley cat
Padded by nonchalantly
You should have seen his eyes
His ears, his whiskers
And his teeth
He was smiling, I'm sure he was
But he only had eyes for "her"
And she was our pure-bred
A Persian, of course

She caught his attention, independent
Lifting a paw to catch his eye
Then she turned away, insultingly
As if to say: Ha! No, you are unworthy!

Quietly, he gazed at her
Tail swishing back and forth
Softly, he moved toward her
Basking in the sunshine and the warm wind

She sat pompously
Licked her coat
Clawed her cushion
Intent on showing her suitor
That beauty has its attractions
And banality, its drawbacks
In this garden she was queen
And he, but a miserable wretch
Was left to blink and sigh longingly

He chose to sit by the door
Not daring to take a step further
Content to stare and admire
To preen calmly and quietly

After two hours of the elaborate game
He disappeared surreptitiously
Seeing her suddenly and impulsively
Running out of the garden
I thought she had lost all control
She had chosen to follow her insolent suitor
Without the slightest hesitation
She had broken free
She had chosen passion!

L.T.

Cats and Plants

You love your cat but he has the bad habit of munching on your house plants, or worse still, of leaving a few odoriferous "surprises" in the soil.

To keep him away without frightening him, cover the soil with a thick coat of peat moss, with pebbles or with clumps of clay. This strategy is effective and much more environment- and animal-friendly than the horrible animal repellents available on today's market.

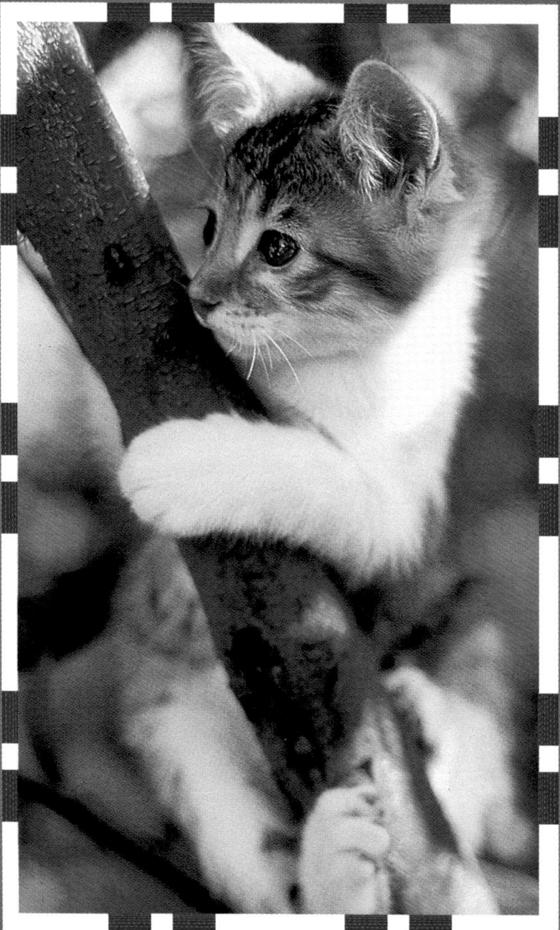

A Cat's Life

I live with my older sister and her cat, Cleopatra. My sister works to earn our living and I go to school. I know she loves me, but sometimes we have **cat-and-dog** arguments. For example, the other day, she was **sunning herself like a cat**, and then she decided to come over to the table where I was writing. For no apparent reason, she said: "You think you're **the cat's meow**, don't you!" I replied: "Not at all. It's not my fault if I'm smart!" But she'd already marched out, looking very haughty and feline indeed.

Luckily I have Cleopatra. When I'm with her, I can say anything, I don't have to be afraid of **letting the cat out of the bag**. I don't feel like **a cat on a hot tin roof**. Sometimes we play **cat and mouse**, but we never disagree.

But things aren't always so much fun — I do have to go to my classes, you know. And when I do, I take along a snack to eat after my **cat nap**. When it's raining **cats and dogs** outside, sometimes we play **cat's cradle** with the younger kids. When the weather is good, we older students can stroll along the **catwalk** and gossip. Sometimes one of us **lets the cat out of the bag**.

When I come home, usually my sister isn't there yet, so I can play with Cleopatra for a while. **When the cat's away the mice will play!** The other day she came home all excited, eager to show me the **cat's-eye** ring she found at a flea market. That **set the cat among the pigeons!** She'd told me she was saving her money to buy me a birthday present... I let out a **catcall**. It just wasn't fair! But after a while I decided not to be **catty**. After all I do love my sister — she's such a kitten!

L.T.

"Earning a cat's friendship is a difficult process. Cats are philosophical, strange, habit-ridden creatures. They love order and cleanliness. They refuse to give love haphazardly. They want to be friends with us (if we should prove to be worthy) but they refuse to be enslaved. They cherish their freedom and they steadfastly resist what they consider to be unreasonable..."

Théophile Gautier

A Feline Delight

"If you want to see what others are unable to see, rub your eyes with cat droppings and chicken fat mixed together in wine."

F. Méry

Of course, this sorcerer's recipe invokes the many superstitions linked with cats and passed down throughout the centuries. But its supposed logic would be much too long to outline here. Instead, the following is a very special recipe that your cat is sure to like... and that you may like yourself!

Fried Liver for Pampered Cats

1. Choose appetizing livers from grain-fed chickens (why not spoil our feline friends).
2. Melt a little butter in a large frying pan.
3. Coat each piece of liver sparingly, in a mixture of bread crumbs and grated parmesan cheese (did you know that cats love cheese?).
4. Sauté for a few minutes, until the liver loses its pink colour.
5. Serve in your cat's prettiest dish.

The advantage of this very simple recipe is that it can double as a meal for humans. Serve with steamed green beans and a hint of Dijon mustard. Enjoy!

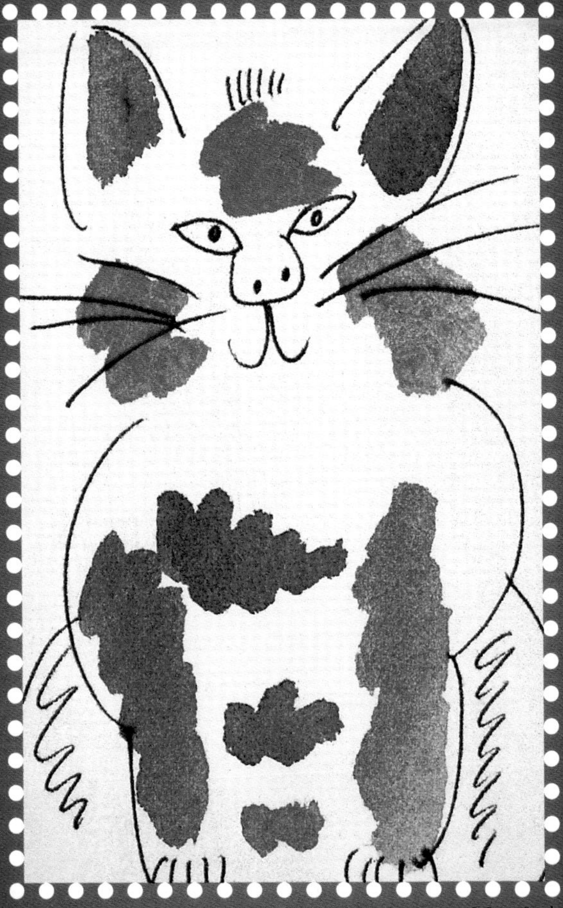

A Feline Legend

One day the prophet Mohammed fell asleep after a long period of meditation on life, death and the importance of things. His favourite cat, Muezza, also slept, tucked into the sleeve of his coat.

The prophet awakened with a start, remembering that people were expecting him and fearing that he would be late. Just before he leaped from his bed, he noticed the beautiful Muezza, softly purring and comfortably resting by his side. Intent on not troubling his feline companion's dreams, he ordered his servant to cut off his sleeve, and then calmly left with no afterthought to his outward appearance.

Upon his return, as a token of her appreciation, the cat bowed before the wisdom of a man willing to bend to the grace and elegance of so lowly a creature.

To express his unshakable affection, Mohammed ran his hand along Muezza's spine three times, smiling at the cat's meows of appreciation and reciprocal affection.

Since that day, according to tales told in every home around the world, cats have the gift of always falling on their feet.

Older Cats

How sad they seem, these older cats
How they miss the laps
They found so warm and welcoming!

How they miss the long evenings
When the soft hands of their owners
Gently caressed their ears and backs!

When they were much-loved kittens
Arching well-fed backs and licking glistening fur
How beloved they seemed to be

They knew wily ways
To sheen their furry paws
Dreaming happily of female companions

Or, like the mighty sphinx
They would purr on luxuriant carpets
Readily giving up the cat-and-mouse chase

No matter clever rodents!
How magic the joy of indulgence
Of sweet milk and soft hands

But oh! a reversal of fortunes!
The scourge of selfish owners
All too ready to banish their former favourites

Now they are gypsies
In the deep of snowy and windblown nights
They shiver and yearn for shelter;

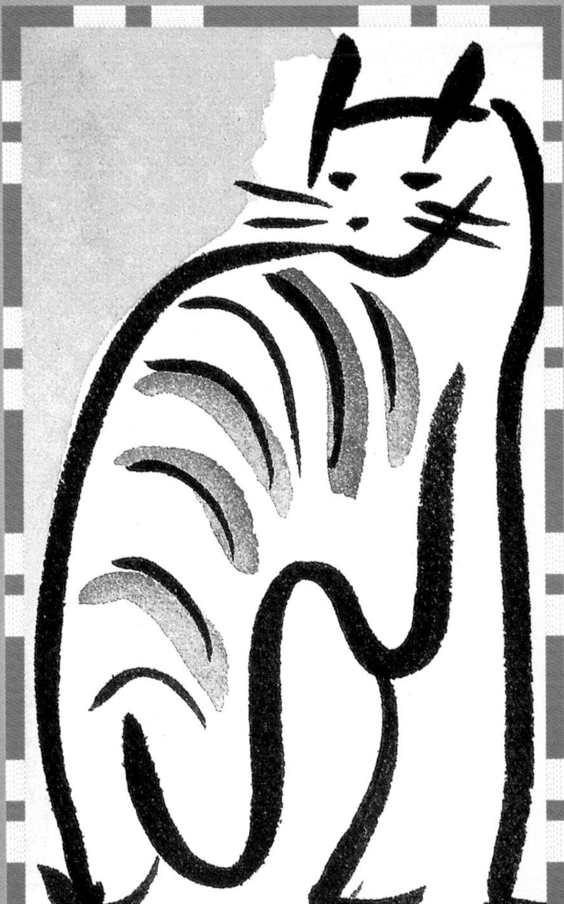

Emaciated and funereal figures,
They are but shadowy profiles
Walking with bent back

And when by chance they see
A kindly figure passing by
Perhaps with a gentle step and smile

They remember the sweetness
Of meals provided with care
They crave what they have lost

These older cats, sad and wandering
Haunted by a bitter need for revenge
Can but howl their sadness.

Raoul Gineste, Poet (1849-1914)

"When my heart seems ready to break
When I choose to speak or write of my pain
Belaud, my small grey kitten...
By chance, Belaud
Nature's most marvellous work
At least when it comes to felines
Belaud comes to mind
And his beauty seems worthy of immortality."
Joachim du Bellay (1522-1560)

Did you know that...

... in Tokyo, the facade of the Go-To-Ku-Ji temple is decorated with cats with one paw raised as a sign of salutation.

... for Egyptians, the goddess Bastet, guardian of light, is associated with the cat.

.... the male cat is the ultimate symbol of passionate love.

... the gender of newborn kittens is a mystery, even for experts, and it remains undetermined for several days, even several weeks, after their birth.

... cats love stuffed olives!

... in Southern Britanny, people believe that black cats have a perfectly white hair hidden somewhere in their fur and that for whoever finds it, it is a lucky charm that lasts throughout a lifetime, as long as it is hidden in a safe place, far away from drafts. Legend has it that this single white hair will make its finder fabulously wealthy and lucky in love for the rest of his or her days.

... the proverb "every cat in the twilight is grey" is universal.

... Madagascar once said: "The rat's movements are not as quick as the brightness in a cat's eyes".

... an Arab proverb says that "a cat once bitten by a snake fears even a simple rope"; in other words, once bitten (by a cat, perhaps), twice shy.

"Cats do not caress us, they use us to caress them."
Rivarol (1753-1801)

My White Cat

I was a small child when my white cat, who liked to venture far afield, came back home with fleas. The tiny insects soon appeared on my mother's bare legs, where our large white cat used to like to go to "caress himself".

When my mother consulted the family doctor, he asked if we had a pet, and then suggested that we get rid of the cat. It was the end of the world. My father went to the veterinarian's and returned with a powder the colour of milk chocolate and instructions to spread it over our cat's fur. On the first attempt, my father only half succeeded in covering the cat with the terrible chestnut-coloured mixture. But Melon (our cat), proud of the pure white colour of his magnificent coat, wasn't easily fooled. As soon as we tried to approach him with the powder container in hand, he ran away as fast as he could. Of course, inevitably he would come back a few hours later, eager to eat his next meal in his special corner of the kitchen. Visibly nervous, eventually he would creep under the dinner table to clean himself quietly.

Unfortunately, my mother's legs were covered with flea bites that were extremely itchy. A few weeks later, our father came up with a solution that pleased no one: we had to get rid of Melon. It was a question of the cat or our mother. Presented in this way, the choice couldn't have been clearer. But the prospect was cruel nonetheless.

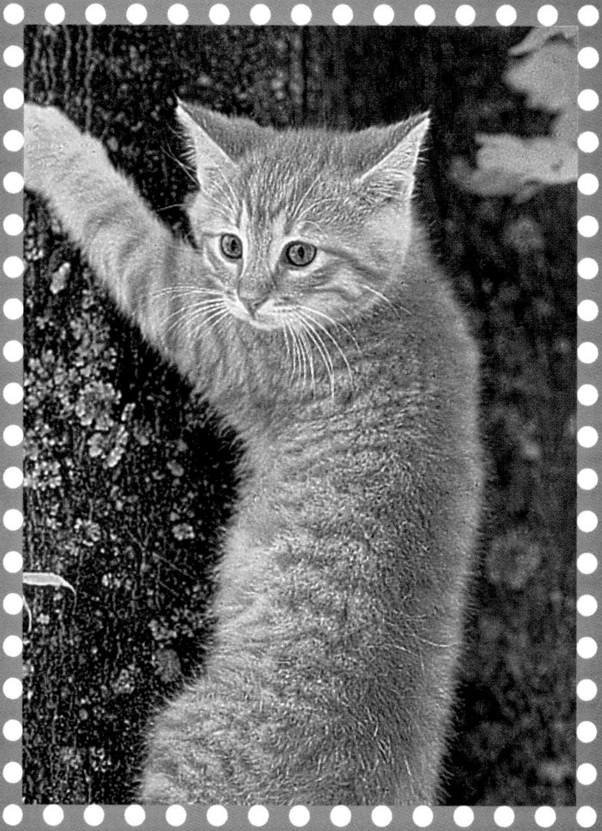

Several months after his "disappearance", I could still see my cat everywhere in the house. When I turned around quickly, I could see him under the table, in all his splendour, quiet and magnificent as ever. I'm sure that what I saw was his spirit, a constant presence that comforted me and hurt me at the same time.

Melon looked every bit as beautiful as ever, but his silent presence seemed to carry blame, and it shattered my little girl's heart. The years went by, I owned other cats, but Melon remained the mythical cat of my childhood, a bittersweet memory, similar to the memory of true love and the torments it can bring.

Surf the Internet for advice and information on cats and other felines. Some of the best sites include:

Veterinary information on cats:
http://www.vetinfo.com/catinfo.html

Cat care video for kids, teaches pet responsibility to children, looks at cat health care:
http://www.yournewkitty.com

On-line feline bookstore:
http://www.hdw-inc.com/felinebookstore1e.htm

The Tiger Foundation:
www.tigerfdn.com and info@tigerfdn.com

Brushing Your Pet

Most cats love being brushed and willingly submit to the process. Long-haired cats like Persians require more care than their short-haired counterparts, mainly because the fur they swallow tends to accumulate in their stomachs. Fur balls lead to vomiting and, in the long run, can lead to serious health problems. So if you have a long-haired cat, brush it often. Your reward will be a healthy, grateful and loving cat!

Spoiling Your Pet

Nepeta cataria is a plant that belongs to the mint family; it is more commonly known as catnip. You can grow it indoors, in a clay pot, or outdoors, during clement weather. Your cat will love it and will happily roll around in it as soon as you give him the opportunity.

If you don't have room to grow it, from time to time buy some catnip at your local pet shop or at a florist's. What better way to show your cat that you love him!

© Private Collection/Christian Pierre/SuperStock

Blue Purple

The cat was blue!
Its daughter was purple!
There they sat
The two of them, side by side
Looking into the trees
And the birds perched on branches
Each in their own world
Yet together
Focused on their prey

Blue and purple
And also dripping wet
Having just emerged from the lake

You won't believe me
After all this was a cat
But its wet black fur
Took on a shiny blue hue
One I saw with my own eyes

To return to my story
The birds, nervous, began to screech
The cats were on the alert
Rogues and villains
Him blue, her purple
With not the blink of an eye
They listened to the twittering
Of the angel-like creatures above
She envied their carefree state
He simply craved the objects of his desire
Her so purple
Him so blue

L. T.

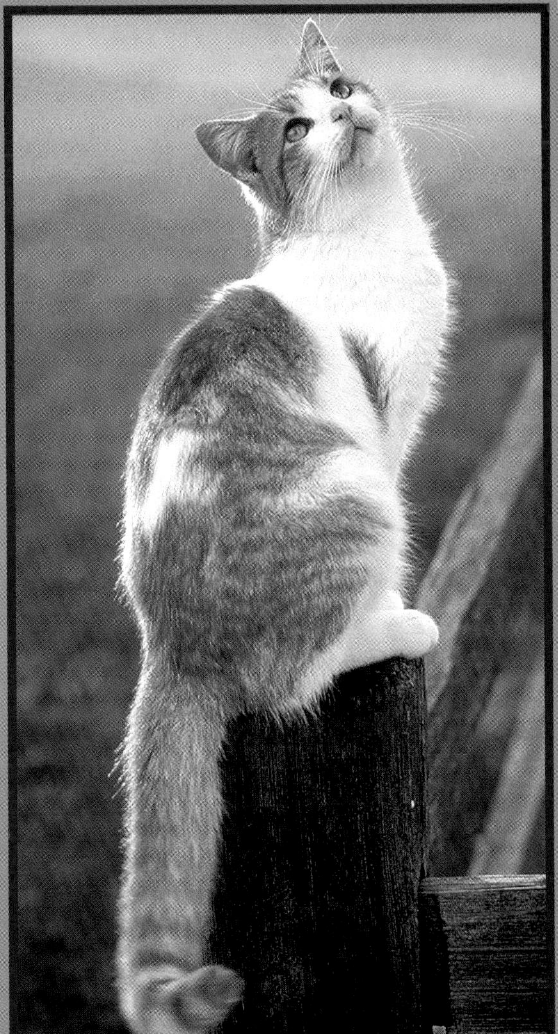

Grooming

When I was a very little girl, my 11-year-old brother had very short hair. Every night, our white cat would creep into my brother's bedroom and jump onto his bed, then gently settle down near the sleeping boy's head. With infinite patience and enjoyment, he would lick my brother's very short hair for a number of minutes, neglecting not a single square inch. Inevitably, after a short while my brother would wake up. But he would always remain motionless — our pet's mark of affection obviously made him feel happy and content.

A bit envious of their intimacy, I begged my mother to cut my hair short. Of course, I never explained the real reason for my request. Surprised and unwilling to give into a demand she regarded as odd, my mother refused categorically.

And so I never experienced the sensation of having my hair lovingly licked by my beloved pet cat.

"The epitome of calm: a cat sitting quietly."
                                        Jules Renard

The Black Cat

(...)
Under the mill, near a stream
Calmly seated in the water
Is an ebony black cat;
She is asleep:
Her eyes are two golden slits
And her claws are tucked away.

But be well aware
As you you swim and gambol about
Golden perch and rainbow trout
Be careful not to stray too close to shore
Lest a furtive claw
Suddenly clutch your back!

Of course, she hates water,
Does this lovely black cat!
But for the pleasure of harpooning
A shiny fresh trout
She is very willing
To get just a little wet
As she swipes her paw into the stream
(...)

(...)
It is midnight, the farm is quiet
All alone, slowly opening her two golden eyes
Nestled close to the fireplace, the old cat
Waits and watches, slowly and steadily
Rubbing her paws along one
And then the other ear.

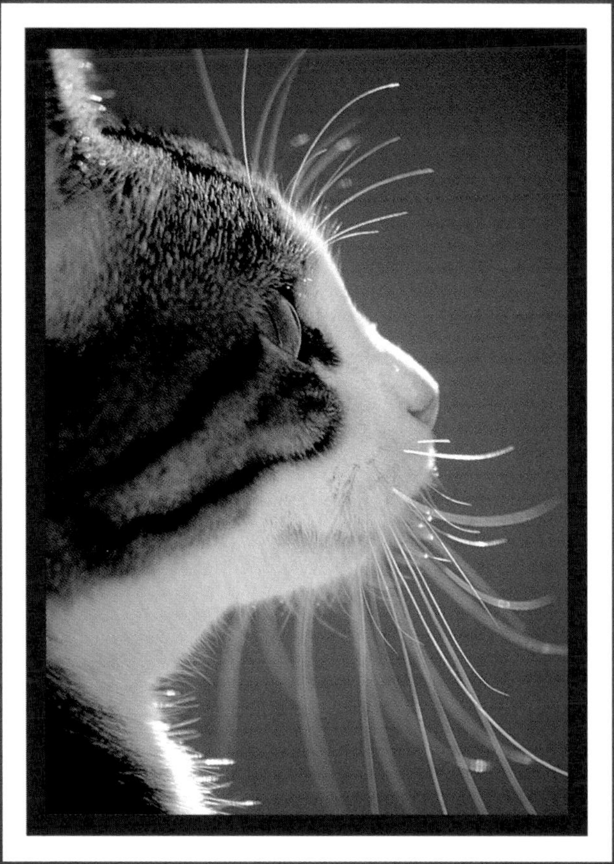

At times she pauses
To look at the burning logs
And embers in the fireplace
Or to listen to the sound
Of the wood as it burns brightly
A sound so like the sound of bird wings.

The master's hunting dog, Lord,
Lies nearby, dreaming of the forest
Yelping softly as he sleeps
And the cat, anxious,
Keeps her eyes half open
Ever ready to fight.

And now her kittens approach
Eager for her love... Devilish paws
Rub against her sleek fur
She warns them off
With a low growl, teeth bared
Angry, playing the stern mother.

At last, with a loud mewl
To each and every one
She handily gives a maternal cuff
And as silence descends
She lies down to let them suckle
Contentedly closing her golden eyes.

François Fabié (excerpt)

Liver Pâté - Marquis de Carabas Style

Cooking time: 1 hour
Preparation time: 20 minutes
Oven temperature: 375°F

$1/2$ to $3/4$ chicken or calves' liver
125 g/4 oz of bacon
2 tablespoons butter
30 g/$1/4$ cup sifted flour
150 ml/$2/3$ cup whole milk
seasoning
1 egg
3 teaspoons minced onion
2 teaspoons port wine
$1/2$ teaspoon salt
$1/2$ teaspoon freshly ground pepper

1. Wash the liver and if necessary, remove any visible veins. Chop very finely and mix with the chopped bacon. Blend in a food processor.
2. Make a thick sauce with the butter, flour, and milk, stirring constantly. Add seasoning.
3. Mix the liver and bacon into the seasoned white sauce and add the beaten egg.
4. Add the onion and the port wine; add the salt and pepper.
5. Place the mixture into a buttered casserole dish.
6. Place the casserole dish in a pan, in approximately one inch of water, and cook until firm (approximately 1 hour).

Served with delicious fresh-baked bread. This pâté is an extraordinary hors d'oeuvre, for you and certainly for your cat! Why not share it — the better to make your pet love you even more!

"La gatta vorrebbe mangiare pesci, ma non pescare!"
"The hungry cat is willing to eat fish, but has no desire to go fishing!"

Italian proverb

Fried Smelt

1 kilo gutted and rinsed smelt
40 g/^{1}/3 cup all-purpose flour
salt and freshly ground pepper
1 egg
1 tablespoon lemon juice
75 g/^{3}/4 cup bread crumbs
dill
3 tablespoons olive oil

1. In a shallow dish, mix together the flour, salt and pepper.
2. In a bowl, beat the egg and lemon juice.
3. Dip the smelt in the flour, the egg mixture, and the bread crumb and dill mixture.
4. Over medium heat, fry in the olive oil.
5. Serve on a bed of lettuce, with baby carrots and lemon slices.

Don't forget to save a portion for your cat — if not, he'll be mad and who could blame him!

Théophile Gautier (1811-1872) tells the story of his cat, Madame Théophile, who experienced the surprise of her life when one fine day, the parrot who shared her house suddenly began to talk.

"*The parrot observed the cat's every movement, obviously febrile; it ruffled its feathers, rattled its chain, lifted one of its legs and showed its claws, and ran its beak along the seed tray. Instinct told it that it was looking at an enemy plotting a coup. The cat's eyes, fascinated and rivetted on the bird, in a language crystal clear and unambiguous to the parrot, said: "Even if you're green, what a delicious bird you seem to be!"*
(...) Madame Théophile drew closer and closer: her pink nose sniffed, her eyes all but closed, her claws poised and withdrew. Small shivers ran up and down her spine; she was a gourmet about to eat the meal of a lifetime; she was savouring the idea of the succulent and rare meal about to be hers. Her exotic dish excited her sensuality. Suddenly, her back arced and with a single bound, she reached the bird's perch. Seeing the imminent peril, in a grave and deep tone, the parrot suddenly cried: "Have you eaten this morning, Jacquot?"
The phrase instantly struck terror in the cat's heart, and helplessly, it fell backwards. A fanfare of bugles, a pile of dishes hurtling to the floor, a gunshot could strike no stronger fear into its heart. All of its ornithological fantasies disappeared. "What did you eat? — A feast fit for a king..." the bird continued. The cat's physiognomy was the perfect expression of its reaction: "This isn't a bird — this is a human, it can speak!"

"When I drink light red wine
I have no need to dine
Life is so, so fine"
the bird sang as loudly as it could. Clearly, its best
defense was terror. The cat looked at us questioningly
and faced with an unsatisfactory response, it fled under
the nearest bed, where it stayed for the rest of the day.
The next morning, Madame Théophile, only slightly
more confident, decided to repeat the scenario. Faced
with the same outcome, she quickly retreated. She was
right: this green creature was indeed some form of
human."

The Owl and the Pussy-Cat

The Owl and the Pussy-Cat went to sea
In a beautiful pea-green boat:
They took some honey, and plenty of money
Wrapped up in a five-pound note.
The Owl looked up to the stars above,
And sang to a small guitar,
"O lovely Pussy-Cat, O Pussy-Cat my love,
What a beautiful Pussy-Cat you are,
You are,
You are!
What a beautiful Pussy-Cat you are!"

Edward Lear

© SuperStock

was a small child when my white cat, who liked to venture far afield,
ack home with fleas. The tiny insects soon appeared on my mother's
gs, where our large white cat used to like to go to "caress himself".
y mother consulted the family doctor, he asked if we had a pet, and
uggested that we get rid of the cat. It was the end of the world. My f
ent to the veterinarian's and returned with a powder the colour of
hocolate and instructions to spread it over the our cat's fur. On the
ttempt, my father only half succeeded in covering the cat with the te
hestnut coloured mixture. But Melon (our cat), proud of the pure

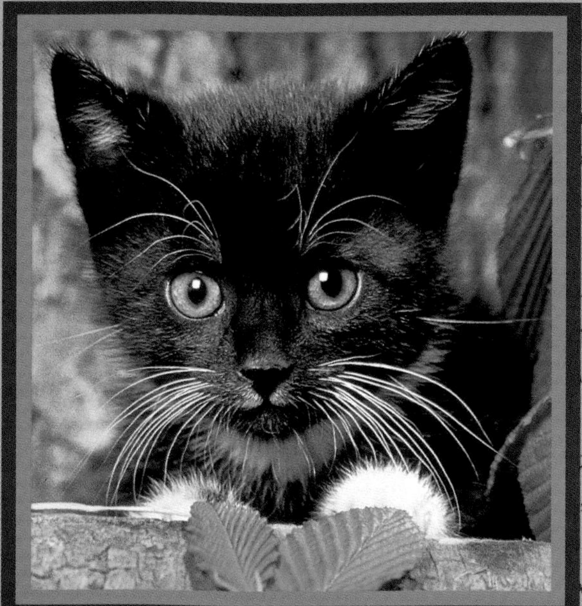

olour o ... e tri
pproac ... fa
e coule ... rs
ager to ... ly
us, eve ... elf
ly. Un ... hat
xtremel ... tion
eased ... f th
r our m ... cle
ut it the ... "di
earanc ... Wh
rned ... s s
our, q ... wo
pirit, a ... me
elon looked every bit as beautiful as ever, but his silent presence se
carry blame, and it shattered my little girl's heart. The years went
ned other cats, but Melon remained the mythical cat of my childho
ttersweet memory, similar to the memory of true love and the torme
n bring. I was a small child when my white cat, who liked to ventur
field, came back home with fleas. The tiny insects soon appeared
other's bare legs, where our large white cat used to like to go to "ca
mself". When my mother consulted the family doctor, he asked if we